# The Massachusetts Colony

K E V I N   C U N N I N G H A M

**Children's Press®**
An Imprint of Scholastic Inc.
New York   Toronto   London   Auckland   Sydney
Mexico City   New Delhi   Hong Kong
Danbury, Connecticut

**Content Consultant**
Jeffrey Kaja, PhD
Associate Professor of History
California State University, Northridge

Library of Congress Cataloging-in-Publication Data

Cunningham, Kevin, 1966–
  The Massachusetts Colony/Kevin Cunningham.
    p. cm.—(A true book)
  Includes bibliographical references and index.
  ISBN-13: 978-0-531-25391-5 (lib. bdg.)      ISBN-13: 978-0-531-26604-5 (pbk.)
  ISBN-10: 0-531-25391-0 (lib. bdg.)      ISBN-10: 0-531-26604-4 (pbk.)
  1. Massachusetts—History—Colonial period, ca. 1600–1775—Juvenile literature. I. Title. II. Series.
  F67.C95 2011                                      974.4'02—dc22

All rights reserved. Published in 2012 by Children's Press, an imprint of Scholastic Inc.
Printed in China 62
SCHOLASTIC, CHILDREN'S PRESS, A TRUE BOOK, and associated logos are trademarks and/or registered trademarks of Scholastic Inc.
1 2 3 4 5 6 7 8 9 10 R 21 20 19 18 17 16 15 14 13 12

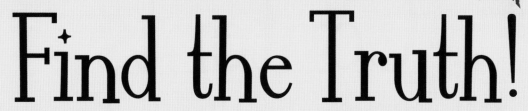

# Find the Truth!

**Everything** you are about to read is true *except* for one of the sentences on this page.

Which one is **TRUE**?

**T or F**    The Pilgrims needed no help to start their colony.

**T or F**    Massachusetts colonists were loyal to Great Britain for a long time.

Find the answers in this book.

# Contents

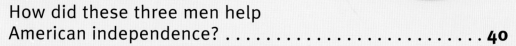

## Massachusetts's Founding Fathers

How did these three men help
American independence? . . . . . . . . . . . . . . . . . . . . . . . . . **40**

The Continental Congress
established the Continental
army on June 14, 1775.

# Timeline of Massachusetts Colony History

**8,000 B.C.E.**

Ancestors of the Wampanoag arrive.

**1620**

The *Mayflower* arrives.

**1675**

King Philip's War begins.

**1773**

Colonists hold the Boston Tea Party.

**1780**

Massachusetts state charter is drafted.

# Pox, Pilgrims, and People of the First Light

The Wampanoag lived in eastern Massachusetts for thousands of years before Europeans arrived to colonize the area. Their name means "people of the first light." They hunted, fished, and practiced **agriculture**. Their main crops were maize (corn), squash, and beans. Women tended the farms and did the sewing. They also turned animal hides into leather and fur clothing. Men hunted animals such as turkeys, deer, and bears. They also fished.

# Wampanoag Life

A successful Wampanoag hunter shared his hunt with less fortunate families. That way everyone in the band survived. Children learned from their parents and older relatives. The girls learned from their mothers. Boys learned from their fathers. Wampanoag made their homes in two kinds of structures. They built rectangular longhouses and wetus, or wigwams. The Wampanoag created mats of woven cattails that they placed over a wooden frame to make the dome-shaped wetu.

**Wetus could be taken apart and put together quickly.**

The Wampanoag lived in different areas during the summer and the winter.

**In 1600, the Wampanoag lived in about 40 villages.**

## The Village

The Wampanoag moved between different locations. They packed up the mats to cover a wetu in their new location. The wooden frame remained standing for use when they returned. The Wampanoag built their villages near good farmland and hunting grounds. Many bands moved to summer villages and then back to wintering areas a short distance away. The villages dotted the Massachusetts coast when European colonists arrived.

Verrazano was killed and eaten by cannibals on a later voyage to the Caribbean.

Giovanni da Verrazano and his men were the first Europeans to visit what is now Massachusetts.

## Exploration by Europeans

Explorer Giovanni da Verrazano, working for France, entered the waters of present-day Rhode Island in 1524 and traded with the Wampanoag. Other European fishing boats and traders soon followed. Some of the traders kidnapped Wampanoag to take back to Europe as slaves. Slave takers raided the village of Patuxet in 1614. One of the captives was Squanto. He was a young Wampanoag training as a special warrior and adviser to Patuxet's sachem, or chief.

Diseases brought by Europeans affected the region's native peoples two years later. Possibly nine out of ten Wampanoag died. So many died that Patuxet was deserted. The fields went untended. This scene greeted the 102 passengers of the *Mayflower* in 1620. The settlers explored the area. They found fresh water but also angry Wampanoag survivors with bows and arrows. They fired their guns to chase off the Indian attackers.

**The *Mayflower* arrived on land on November 21, 1620.**

# The Pilgrims

The settlers are known today as the Pilgrims. They had fled religious **persecution** in England. Their new colony allowed them to practice their faith as they wished. But they had no idea how to survive in the new land. Close to half the Pilgrims died during the winter. The rest barely survived on food the Wampanoag had buried years earlier and the little food they had brought with them. It took until the next spring for them to finish turning Patuxet into a Pilgrim town called New Plimoth.

**The winter months were extremely difficult for the Pilgrims.**

The Pilgrims probably ate geese and ducks at the first Thanksgiving.

Thanksgiving became a national holiday in the United States in 1863.

The local Wampanoag sachem was named Massasoit. He soon made contact. Massasoit brought with him a man who spoke English. Squanto had learned the language in Europe. He had returned home after acquiring his freedom. He taught the Pilgrims the Wampanoag ways of farming and survival. In the fall, the two peoples shared a feast remembered today as Thanksgiving. New Plimoth grew in the years that followed. But starting in 1630, another colony would eclipse it.

MAINE
(PART OF
MASSACHUSETTS)

Area
enlarged

Original
13 Colonies

ATLANTIC OCEAN

NEW YORK

VERMONT
(CLAIMED BY
NEW HAMPSHIRE
AND NEW YORK)

NEW HAMPSHIRE

*Merrimack River*

*Connecticut River*

Deerfield •

Salem •

*Massachusetts
Bay*

Concord •  Lexington •
Cambridge •
Boston •

*Berkshire Hills*

MASSACHUSETTS

Plymouth •

*Cape
Cod
Bay*

CONNECTICUT

RHODE
ISLAND

WAMPANOAG

*Cape Cod*

*Buzzards Bay*

*Nantucket
Sound*

*Martha's
Vineyard*

*Nantucket
Island*

*Long Island*

| miles | |
|---|---|
| 0 | 20 |
| 0 | 20 |
| km | |

——— Colonial boundaries

# CHAPTER 2

# The New Colony

The Puritans were another religous group that
sought to worship in peace. Their **charter** from
England allowed them land and self-government.
More than 300 ships carrying 21,000 people
arrived in New England between 1630 and 1640.
Most of them were Puritans. John Winthrop was
the leader of the first group. He became the first
governor of Massachusetts Bay Colony and had a
say in selecting Boston as the colonial capital.

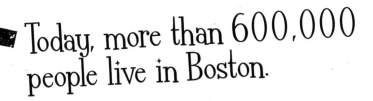

Today, more than 600,000
people live in Boston.

# Puritan Rules

The Puritans lived by strict rules designed to keep their minds focused on God. An elected official called the tithing man made sure people only traveled on Sunday to attend church. People who dressed in fancy clothes were fined. Activities such as dancing and horseshoes were forbidden. The Puritans even disliked play for children. They believed it led to misbehavior. Anyone who challenged the Puritans was thrown out of the colony.

**Puritans strictly enforced their many rules.**

Most Puritan schools consisted of only one room.

## The Schoolhouse

The Puritans valued learning because people needed to read to study the Bible. They passed a law in 1647 that required towns with at least 50 homes to open a schoolhouse. The cold buildings usually had a single stove for heat. Students sat on planks. Girls learned reading, writing, and a little math. Boys might be taught enough Greek and Latin to attend the colony's secondary school in Boston.

# Make What You Need

Goods brought from England were expensive. Massachusetts colonists balanced imported goods with homegrown and homemade ones. Farmers raised sheep in addition to food crops. Women and children spun the sheep's wool into yarn for clothing. Beef fat provided tallow used in soap and somewhat smelly candles. Fish oil was used as fuel for lamps, as was whale oil starting in the 1700s.

# Hard Work

The Puritans divided work into specific tasks for women and men. Women cared for the home. They took charge of cooking, sewing, soap making, and gardening. Raising the children also kept women very busy. Colonial women had big families. They often had six or more children. Children helped with chores once they were old enough. These chores included fetching water from wells or streams, milking the cows, herding sheep, and baking bread.

**Much of the work on family farms was done by children.**

Boys often worked with their fathers, while girls worked with their mothers.

Men worked various jobs. Farming was essential to the Massachusetts **economy**. Trades (specialized jobs) became more important as towns and cities grew in the 1700s. Coopers made barrels. Cobblers made shoes. Tanners made leather. A boy wanting to work in a trade served as an **apprentice** for a period of time learning the skills. Church responsibilities often took up men's time and energy.

During colonial times, goods were made by hand.

Colonists destroyed Native American crops during King Philip's War.

**King Philip's War was the most violent event to occur in New England in the 17th century.**

## Colony at War

The Puritans didn't have the same respect for Native Americans that the Pilgrims did. They took land when they wanted it. The Puritans refused to believe that Indians had complaints worth listening to. The Native Americans began to fight back. Conflict with native peoples in King Philip's War (1675–1676) damaged or destroyed half of the 90 or so towns in New England and killed 600 settlers. More than 3,000 Native Americans died. Only 400 Wampanoag survived when the war ended.

**King Charles II continued to seek ways to get money from the colonies for England.**

# Takeover by England

The war battered Massachusetts's economy. The colony faced an even greater challenge soon after it ended. King Charles II thought the English government should make more money from colonial furs, lumber, and other goods. England revoked the colonial charter in 1684. This took away the colony's right to govern itself. England had taken more control over the colony.

Massachusetts soon regained control of its affairs. But fear and uncertainty were in the air. Wild accusations of witchcraft took over the town of Salem. This led to the Salem witch trials in 1692. A special court had executed 20 falsely accused "witches" and put 150 people in prison by the time it all ended.

The Massachusetts governor's wife was one of the women accused of witchcraft.

Accusations of witchcraft began after a group of young girls began screaming, throwing things, and making strange sounds.

During the 18th century, Boston grew rapidly from a small town into a major port city.

# New Century, New Directions

The colonists had made the New England wilderness into a region of prosperous towns and farms by the beginning of the 1700s. Large families and more **immigrants** helped the colony's population grow to 16,000 in 1740. Boston had become a bustling port that dealt in goods from all across the American colonies. But growing tension between English colonies and a growing French presence in North America would soon cause problems.

← Many of Boston's colonial buildings still stand today.

# Loyalty to Britain

Success and wealth caused many people in Massachusetts to throw off Puritan rules and beliefs. Money now went to expensive waistcoats, silk, and powdered wigs. Shoes with buckles became high fashion, just as in Great Britain. Colonists for the most part considered themselves British. They decorated their houses in British styles. They began to drink tea. It had once been too expensive for colonists to buy. Tea would play a colorful role in Massachusetts's future.

**Large trading ships were a common sight in Boston Harbor.**

There are 34 small islands in Boston Harbor.

During the French and Indian War, colonial militias learned about British military tactics.

Ongoing wars between Britain and France for control over North America tested Massachusetts's loyalty. But the colonists sided with Britain again and again. In 1745, 4,000 members of the Massachusetts **militia** helped take Louisburg. Louisburg was an important French fort that guarded a major river route into North America. War with France erupted again nine years later. Colonial militiamen fought alongside British redcoats and learned the British army's professional way of soldiering. That knowledge would play a role in Massachusetts's future.

**The colonists were enraged when they learned about the Stamp Act.**

## The Issue of Taxes

Protecting the American colonies from French attacks had cost Britain a great deal of money. The British government started creating new taxes in 1764 to help cover the cost. The Sugar Act (1764) tried to control smugglers who brought in tax-free sugar and molasses. The much-hated Stamp Act (1765) forced colonists to buy a stamp for all printed materials such as newspapers and playing cards.

The colonists did not mind all taxes. But they felt they should not be taxed when they had no representatives in the British Government to defend their interests. They called this taxation without representation. **Boycotts** of some British goods began. So did protests in the streets. British merchants began losing money as the colonists refused to buy their goods. Their complaints soon convinced the British to cancel the taxes on all the goods, except tea.

**Colonists protested by burning stamps.**

British leaders hoped that the new tax acts would pay for at least half of the debt from fighting France.

## Massacre and Tea Party

On March 5, 1770, an angry disagreement between Bostonians and British soldiers ended with five colonists dead and 11 wounded. An anti-British pamphlet called the event "a horrid **massacre**." A patriot movement arguing for freedom from Britain had sprung up around the colonies by then. Bostonian Samuel Adams was one of its leading figures. Adams set up a system of supporters called the Sons of Liberty to carry up-to-date news about Britain's poor treatment of colonists to villages throughout Massachusetts.

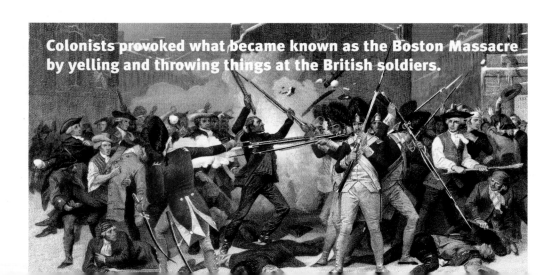

Colonists provoked what became known as the Boston Massacre by yelling and throwing things at the British soldiers.

About 90,000 pounds (40,900 kilograms) of tea were thrown into the harbor.

The events of December 16, 1773, became known as the Boston Tea Party.

The Tea Act was enacted in 1773 to support a struggling British tea company. Tea was to be shipped directly to the colonies and sold at reduced prices. Patriots thought it was a trick forcing them to buy only British tea because of its cheaper price compared to other teas. About 60 of the Sons of Liberty boarded three tea ships on December 16. They tossed 342 tea chests into Boston Harbor. Patriots cheered the raid. The angry British government closed Boston Harbor. What happened next would lead to **revolution**.

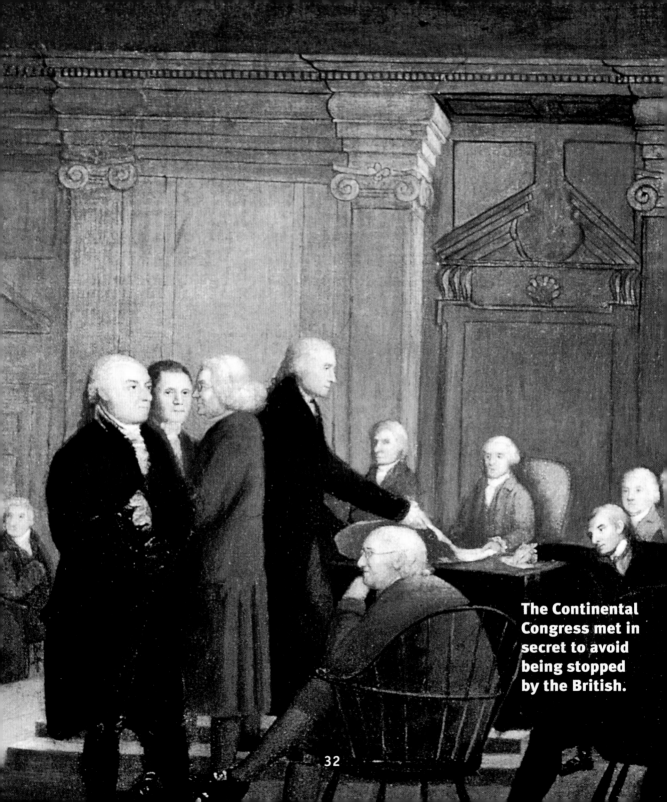

The Continental Congress met in secret to avoid being stopped by the British.

CHAPTER  4

# Revolution and Statehood

Boston's closed port threatened to ruin its economy.
Boston could not bring in foreign goods to sell
in the colonies or ship American goods to sell in
other countries. Representatives from twelve of
the colonies met in Philadelphia for a Continental
Congress. The first task for the Congress was to
decide how to respond to the British government.
The members agreed to boycott British goods and
to refuse to sell American products to Britain.

 Fifty-six men participated in the
First Continental Congress.

33

# The Shot Heard Round the World

Concord, west of Boston, organized a 400-man militia that included 100 minutemen. These were soldiers who could be "ready in a minute." British troops moved on Concord to capture the colonists' military supplies on April 18, 1775. A Boston silversmith named Paul Revere rode ahead to warn of the attack. Minutemen lined up to face the British at Lexington. They fell back when they saw that they were outnumbered A shot rang out, and the British fired. Eight minutemen were killed.

**No one knows who fired the shot that began the American Revolution.**

**Although Britain won the Battle of Bunker Hill, they suffered significant loses.**

Colonists had moved the supplies out of Concord. The British turned back for Boston. Colonial sharpshooters killed 73 soldiers and wounded 174 more. The British found themselves surrounded by militia from all over New England when they returned to Boston.

It took two months for more redcoats to arrive. About 1,200 colonials met them at the Battle of Bunker Hill. The British were trapped in Boston when the fighting ended.

# A Second Congress

In March 1776, British troops fled the colony on ships when they were forced out by colonial militiamen. The Second Continental Congress met in May. All the colonies were asked to create their own governments and to organize a single Continental army to fight Britain. On June 11, the congress chose five people to draft a declaration of independence explaining why the colonies must break from Britain. One of the five people was Massachusetts lawyer John Adams.

(From left to right) Thomas Jefferson, Roger Sherman, Benjamin Franklin, Robert R. Livingston, and John Adams all helped create the Declaration of Independence.

# John Adams

John Adams was one of
the most important of
the Founding Fathers.
He was a teacher
and lawyer before
he became well
known for opposing
the Stamp Act.
He had a hand in
most of the major
government decisions
from the First Continental
Congress through the end of
the revolution. He served twice as
vice president and once as U.S. president after the
United States was founded. He died on July 4, 1826,
the same day as his close friend, Thomas Jefferson.

Thousands of Massachusetts men fought in the Continental army in the American Revolution.

# Declaration of Independence

On July 4, John Adams, along with Samuel Adams and Robert Treat Paine, voted for the declaration for Massachusetts. A fourth representative named Elbridge Gerry added his signature later. The war moved away from Massachusetts soil. No other battles were fought there. But Massachusetts supplied thousands of soldiers for the Continental army. Thousands of other men manned colonial ships battling the powerful British navy. Women worked the farms and maintained businesses in the men's absence.

The Declaration of Independence was read aloud by George Washington to his army.

Towns across Massachusetts agreed on a new state **constitution** in 1780. Fighting stopped in 1781 with the British defeat at Yorktown. The Treaty of Paris officially ended the war in 1783. By 1785, it became clear the former colonies needed a stronger national government in addition to the individual state constitutions. Representatives discussed and argued about the document from May to September 1787. The new U.S. Constitution then went to each state for a vote. On February 16, 1788, Massachusetts voted yes and became the sixth state to join the United States.

# Massachusetts's Founding Fathers

The British king wanted to punish Massachusetts after the Boston Tea Party for ruining so much valuable tea. The "Intolerable Acts" (1774) allowed British troops to demand food and housing from colonists. The acts also took away the colonists' power to elect officials and forbade colonial courts from trying British soldiers for crimes committed in America. They also closed down Boston's port. The acts made it much easier for Massachusetts's patriots to stir up support for independence.

# Samuel Adams

Second cousin to John Adams, Samuel argued for colonial rights as early as 1763. The British occupation of his hometown of Boston led him to support independence. He was one of the first to defend the destruction of tea in Boston Harbor in 1773.

# John Hancock

Hancock was the creator of the most famous signature on the Declaration of Independence. He used his family's fortune to support independence. He served as president of the Second Continental Congress and later was governor of Massachusetts.

# Paul Revere

Revere became famous for his 1775 midnight ride to warn Massachusetts towns of approaching British troops. But Revere had already spent years contributing to pro-independence newspapers and being active in the Sons of Liberty.

The war hurt Massachusetts's economy. But it recovered quickly. Boston remained the major seaport in New England. A number of farmers and merchants had made fortunes selling supplies to the Continental army. Boston had grown to a city of nearly 25,000 people by 1800. John Adams became the second U.S. president in 1797. His election reflected the important role Massachusetts had played in creating the new country and securing American liberty. ★

**By 1800, Boston had begun to look like the modern city it is today.**

# True Statistics

**Number of passengers on board the *Mayflower*:** 102

**Number of people who moved to New England between 1630 and 1640:** 21,000

**Number of Native Americans killed in King Philip's War:** More than 3,000

**Number of people executed for witchcraft in Salem:** 20

**Population of Massachusetts in 1700:** 6,700

**Population of Massachusetts in 1740:** 16,000

**Number of colonists killed in the Boston Massacre:** 5

**Number of tea chests thrown into Boston Harbor:** 342

**Number of minutemen at Concord:** 100

**Number of colonial troops at the Battle of Bunker Hill:** About 1,200

**Number of Massachusetts signers of the Declaration of Independence:** 4

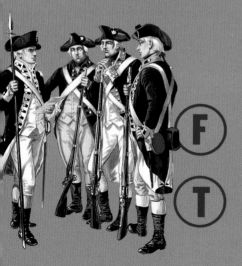

## Did you find the truth?

**F** The Pilgrims needed no help to start their colony.

**T** Massachusetts colonists were loyal to Great Britain for a long time.

# Resources

## Books

DeKeyser, Stacy. *The Wampanoag*. New York: Franklin Watts, 2005.

Dell, Pamela. *The Plymouth Colony*. Mankato, MN: Capstone, 2004.

Hinman, Bonnie. *The Massachusetts Bay Colony: The Puritans Arrive From England*. Hockessin, DE: Mitchell Lane, 2007.

January, Brendan. *Colonial Life*. New York: Children's Press, 2000.

Leotta, Joan. *Massachusetts*. New York: Children's Press, 2008.

Uschan, Michael V. *Lexington and Concord*. New York: Gareth Stevens, 2004.

Whitehurst, Susan. *A Plymouth Partnership: Pilgrims and Native Americans*. New York: PowerKids Press, 2002.

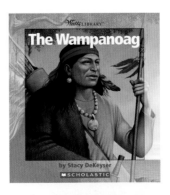

# Organizations and Web Sites

### The Mayflower Society
www.themayflowersociety.com/pilgrim.htm
Learn about the Pilgrims and find good resources at this site provided by people whose ancestors arrived on the *Mayflower*.

### PBS: We Shall Remain: After the Mayflower
www.pbs.org/wgbh/amex/weshallremain/the_films /episode_1_trailer
Watch a documentary about Native Americans in New England during the colonial era.

# Places to Visit

### Commonwealth Museum
220 Morrissey Boulevard
Boston, MA 02125
(617) 727-9268
www.sec.state.ma.us/sec /mus/museum/index.htm
Study exhibits to learn the history of Massachusetts from its early days through the revolution.

### Concord Museum
200 Lexington Road
Concord, MA 01742
(978) 369-9763
www.concordmuseum.org
Enjoy artifacts from the American Revolution and reenactments of historical events at this museum in Concord, Massachusetts.

# Important Words

**agriculture** (AG-ri-kuhl-chur) — the raising of crops and animals

**apprentice** (uh-PREN-tis) — a person who learns a skill by working with an expert

**boycotts** (BOI-kahtz) — refusals to buy goods from a person, group, or country

**charter** (CHAHR-tur) — a formal document guaranteeing rights or privileges

**constitution** (kahn-sti-TOO-shun) — the laws of a country that state the rights of the people and the powers of government

**economy** (ih-KA-ne-mee) — the system of buying, selling, and making things and managing money

**immigrants** (IM-uh-gruhntz) – people who move from one country to another and settle there permanently

**massacre** (MA-suh-kur) — the violent killing of a large number of people at the same time

**militia** (muh-LISH-uh) — a group of people who are trained to fight but who aren't professional soldiers

**persecution** (pur-suh-KYOO-shuhn) — the cruel and unfair treatment of a person because of that person's ideas or beliefs

**revolution** (rev-uh-LOO-shuhn) — open and armed fighting against a government

# Index

Page numbers in **bold** indicate illustrations

# About the Author

Kevin Cunningham has written more than 40 books on disasters, the history of disease, Native Americans, and other topics. Cunningham lives near Chicago with his wife and young daughter.